Dipped in Black Water

New Women's Voices Series, No. 134

poems by

Kate Peper

Finishing Line Press
Georgetown, Kentucky

Dipped in Black Water

New Women's Voices Series, No. 134

Copyright © 2017 by Kate Peper
ISBN 978-1-63534-228-4 First Edition
All rights reserved under International and Pan-American Copyright Conventions.
No part of this book may be reproduced in any manner whatsoever without written permission from the publisher, except in the case of brief quotations embodied in critical articles and reviews.

ACKNOWLEDGMENTS

Grateful acknowledgment is made to the editors of the journals who first published the following poems. These poems were published, sometimes in a variant form or under a different title, as follows:

The Baltimore Review: "The Weight of a Bridge"
Cimarron Review: "End of the Line"
Cultural Weekly: "The Empty Lot," "The Lock Picker," "Later, She Learned He Married and Had a Child"
Great River Review: "Barbie's Secret"
The Lindenwood Review: "The Serial Killer's Parents, Afterward," "Diagnosis," "I Was Not Mistaken"
Ouroboros Review: "Textbook of Pathology"
Poet Lore: "View from the Jungfraujoch Railway Café"
The Potomac Review: "Art Class, Dark Birds"
Quiddity: "The Anointed"
Rattle: "Saved"
Rust + Moth: "Holes"
Spillway: "Photo of a Slice of an Infant's Face"
Tar River Poetry: "The Way It Is"
Seminary Ridge Review: "Ikea"
Windhover: "Hearing My Master's Voice"

"The Serial Killer's Parents, Afterward" was nominated for a Pushcart Prize.

Publisher: Leah Maines
Editor: Christen Kincaid
Cover Art: Kate Peper/www.peperprojects.com©
Author Photo: Marybeth Adkins/Natural Light Photography©
        www.naturallightphoto.com
Cover Design: Kate Peper

Printed in the USA on acid-free paper.
Order online: www.finishinglinepress.com
        also available on amazon.com

Author inquiries and mail orders:
Finishing Line Press
P. O. Box 1626
Georgetown, Kentucky 40324
U. S. A.

Table of Contents

Self Portrait as a Bell 1
Barbie's Secret 2
Textbook of Pathology 3
I Was Not Mistaken 4
End of the Line 5
Swiss Border Town in the Time of War 6
The Way It Is 7
XX 8
First Sex After the Operation to Create My Vagina 9
View from the Jungfrau Railway Café 10
Photo of a Slice of an Infant's Face 11
Stone Baby 12
The Serial Killer's Parents, Afterward 13
The White, High-Ceilinged Room 14
Art Class, Dark Birds 15
Later, She Learned He Married and Had a Child 16
The Weight of a Bridge 17
Holes 18
Diagnosis 19
The Anointed 20
Where Did My Mind Go? 21
Hearing My Master's Voice 22
The Lock Picker 23
Ikea 24
The Empty Lot 25
Saved 26
Notes 27

For God, who made me who I am

Self Portrait as a Bell

We remember the air pricked with whistles and applause as we made way for the truck ferrying the church's new bell. Even the square's sycamores fanned their leaves as if in alleluia. The bell was hoisted and bolted in—nothing but gleam. We looked up, eager for its first peal. The mayor pulled the rope: the bell swung right, left, right—a string of damp sounds that neither sang nor echoed.

The mayor and a swarm of officials stampeded up the belfry. One by one they stood under its iron skirt. Fissures were found not seen from the outside. The clapper was mute, yet one woman was sure it shuddered at her touch. Others put their ear to the cool metal and swore they heard a river.

Though beautiful, the bell has a lopsided sound ring and a lip too cracked for clear pitch, read the Gazette. Without fanfare, the bell was brought down and housed in the museum next to the town's first fire truck.

No one touches it, yet year after year some unseen flaw continues to weaken the bell's ribs. Everyone knows the bell will crack clean through one day and give way altogether. Then a sound, such an unbearable sound.

Barbie's Secret

Barbie never healed
from my ear-piercing attempts,
spearing her tiny lobes
with my mother's sewing pins,
sharp ends exiting opposite cheeks.

I want to cut off her hair—
shear her golden halo to cornstalk bristles,
test the truth of my sister's warning,
a doll's hair won't grow back.

I wonder if her head echoes with voices
telling her to stand straight,
take smaller bites
and cross her legs.
I want to know if she was born
to perfection, a secret safely lodged
between pin-pricked ears.

Barbie floats headless
in my bath, a bubbled heaven
where a body beautiful as hers goes.

She's as smooth as a stone,
her sex blank as a page.
Nippleless breasts glide like islands.
My own, just starting to bead
and rise in cool air.

Textbook of Pathology

Papa calls it the Bible of Disease.
I play hide and seek
with the black and white plates,
memorize where the harelip
and cleft palate boys are.

I wonder why the people
have blanked-out eyes.
Some are my own age,
with lobster hands and spindle legs.

Here's the boy
who died an old man at thirteen.
Progeria, my father says.
The kid is bald, crawling
on all fours.

My father takes the book away
as always, but I'll return
to look at death

stooped in her dark room
stitching a gown for me.
One day, I'll grow into it.

I Was Not Mistaken

There was a way of living in the woods with pines overhead and needles sloughed off and the sun almost blocked out except a finger of light on the bluebells and my bare knees, pressed into the loam as I studied mushrooms the size of stubbed pencils with grey gills and moss like green cloud formations over the mushy log and a daddy-longlegs stepped from softness to softness onto the back of my hand and car sounds and kitchen sounds far away and no one wanted me or knew who I was anymore and maybe this went on for years and the teacher was wrong when she said, *You have an emptiness inside* when I drew that picture of the oak with a hole in its trunk because I know that's where the squirrel lives who eats the acorn and drops it too.

End of the Line

My German great uncle lost all
five sons in WWII, placed
the telegrams with their photos
between pages of the family Bible:
We will endure as God wills.
Five gold stars on the jamb.

One aunt survived two husbands,
had no children.
In her wingback chair
she told my mother exactly
where all she owned would go:
*My spirit to Heaven, everything
else is labeled.* Under each lamp,
porcelain bird, and bookend,
a name on a piece of tape.

At eighteen, I learned
I couldn't have children.
On a plastic torso the doctor
covered the uterus and vagina
with his palm and said,
*These parts are missing,
but you have functioning ovaries.*

I didn't hear his voice after that,
just imagined each egg released
into her own dark passage,
entering a terminal without lights,
with no one to meet her.

Swiss Border Town in the Time of War
—for my mother

the time of happiness as a private matter is

over, Hitler rants on the kitchen radio

    shards of music crackle with static,

        cow brains sizzle

    in sardine oil saved

from the tin

    her mother boils coffee made from chicory,

        from acorns, from dust

        she wraps an orange in a towel:

close your eyes and make-believe

    we have a birthday cake for you

        the girl closes her eyes and makes

her wish: *red shoes*

    for one day, red shoes.

The Way It Is
> *In her dream, she rides backward on an ass into a cave painted with vaginas.*

Girls are ready for Crest White Strips at 13,
because a woman's wealth is in her smile.

The unhappiness of a childless woman
is measured in cats.

Every girl loves horses:
All that power held between her legs.

Women afraid to ride horses
dream they'll birth kittens.

If a girl's born on a Sunday,
she'll own two pairs of riding boots.

If a girl's born at midnight,
she'll suffer confusion.

When you bleed, you become a woman.
Women who don't bleed are witches.

XX

Goya painted *Saturn Devouring His Son*
on his living room wall.
The child's head already gone,
her left arm lit by blood.

*Because you were born without
a vagina and uterus,* the doctor said,
*your eggs will be freed
into the body and absorbed.*

Every month I felt the cramping
I thought of that painting.
With every stab of an egg's release,
I was erasing myself:
Pearls down a blood river.

At twenty, I found a surgeon who could carve
the flesh between my legs,
making my closed hole open.
Yet the nurse who checks on my healing
asks, Why? You still can't have babies.

Where there was nothing
I now have something.
I tell her, *This is how I begin
to feel whole.*

First Sex After the Operation to Create My Vagina

                  You pull me into your cabin and strip me
        in the dark,
the woosh of the toilet
        endlessly filling—

When you penetrated me, everything opened:
      my new vagina blossomed,
            the black barked trees shook with pale petals,
the deer outside stayed: the buck swayed his antlered head,
      the doe got wet up to her belly from the unmown
         and drizzled grasses.

View From the Jungfraujoch Railway Café

She lights another
and orders a second *kaffee crème*
because she's on holiday.

Outside, blond children flock
to viewfinders; zoom in
on the Eiger and the body

swinging like an uneven pendulum,
metal clips glinting on his pack
as he knocks and knocks against the rock.

*Maybe they'll bring him down
in summer,* says the waiter,
when the winds aren't so bad.

The woman stubs out her cigarette,
walks outside and stops
next to the kids.

She thinks about the moment
his frostbitten fingers let go,
his body plunging unseen,

his shout unheard by tourists
sipping coffee, the Bernese Alps
a furnace of gold in the afternoon sun.

Photo of a Slice of an Infant's Face

1.
Better not to give a name
or know its history. Or think of it
as human once. Better to thank
the scientist who carved it
thin as a bee's wing. Thank him
for his fine control of the tweezers,
for dyeing the slice, backlighting it
under glass.

2.
Flat as a map, ragged edges of a landmass
in a black sea. Humidity and wonder.
Long-ago lakes—the toothless mouth,
the crater of an eye, between them
the harbor of a nose.
Ear, a tide pool dyed deep red.
Rain on a screen door,
tick of a clock.

3.
List on a white dresser:
Anna, Lily, Claire. Others
crossed out. Ashes
of a spirit that blinked
and couldn't quite cross over.

Stone Baby
> *A 44-year old lithopedion fetus has been found in an 84-year old Brazilian woman. [The woman] says she does not want the fetus removed.* —USA Today, 2014

For decades you hid within her but outside
the womb, grew life-like but refused air,

stayed curled, thumb-sucking
homunculus, wrapped in a calcium shell.

When they showed your never-to-be
mother your grey image,

she touched the CT screen and gasped,
Lua Nova: My new moon dipped in black water.

Her old knees have buckled
with your weight.

No, she said to the surgeon. To keep you
she will crawl with her big belly if she must:

*God's lamp shone here
and still does.*

The Serial Killer's Parents, Afterward

Cracking the morning silence with an egg
in the new town. Cream to lighten
his coffee, his *good morning* make-believe.

Their new name hasn't sunk in,
doesn't feel right in their mouths.

She pretends to plan raised beds
for winter vegetables. Neither
would dream of getting a pet.

Come spring, she'll hang a new birdhouse.
He'll paint the fence white
to show they belong.

The White, High-Ceilinged Room

The hydrocephalic boy rests in bed.
Everyone entering must remove their shoes:
clicking or tapping hurts his ears.

His parents carry him to a basin
and pour warm water
over the dry leaf of his body.
His mother hums.
The boy closes his eyes
imagining Heaven:

He will run, feel his weight
against the wind, his tennis shoes
drumming the earth.

Father helps him stand
while Mother towels him off,
My, your nails have grown.
We'll have to cut them!
Her words are drowned
in the ocean inside his head.

He feels his skull separating,
seams between bone plates weakening.
Soon, his head will open like a flower,
the Earth whole below him.

Art Class, Dark Birds

Riffling magazine pages, soft ripping
of paper, sunlit room.
My friend killed herself last week, she says,
in the room below mine.
No one found her for days.

Our eyes look up, dart down.
A pause, then glue sticks glide again.
A woman next to her whispers, *Oh my.*
I'm so sorry…Could you pass the scissors?

Our collages feature smiling children,
and archways adorned by camellias.
Her voice again:
I love crows; they remind me of her.
I should have known something was wrong
when I kept seeing so many circling our house.

I glance over to where she sits
tearing out dark birds,
evening gowns, night skies.
She murmurs,

My friend left a note, "No one loves me
except my grandmother, and she's dead."
She pauses to rest her fingertips
in the hollow of her throat,

then goes back to her black-
on-black collage, not one white corner
open.

Later, She Learned He Married and Had a Child

She thought of the marriage
she almost had, how the ring
made it seem true and their holiday
that summer on Lake Michigan,
feeding each other black cherries in bed.
His kisses left dark stains on her neck
she did not want to rub off.

On their last evening
they stood on the coarse sand
and watched something black,
round, float in the waves.
Let's guess, she entreated.
A lost seal? Or a selkie?
It bobbed in place as if tethered
to some invisible weight.
She turned to him, *No, a child!*

He started back to their rented cabin,
turned and called, *Are you coming?*
She shook her head, stood watching
the waves drain of color.
It's just a broken pylon, he said,
unlacing his fingers from hers.

The Weight of a Bridge

made so much heavier by pigeon shit,
the slow accretion and stink of it all.
Generations of bland-eyed birds
with softly fluorescent wings fanning
as they alighted, shat, cooed.

Nobody guessed they could crush a bridge
over time, or how the brass balls of the Wall Street Bull
would be so shiny from all the years of hands touching,
the testicles some totem of luck or fortune
made smaller year by year—
the way our great love was reduced
to that last day we met by the Mississippi.

Spring, the Russian olives mad with perfume.
The moment you said *over*
the dead dog came into view,
draped over the rock in the river, hair worn off,
skin obsidian, lapped by water.

Holes

I used to sit in the hole
in our tire swing.
When the rope rotted, Papa and I

drove to a graveyard of old tires
and heaved it, re-tread flying.
Driving home past the row

of No Smoking signs,
he said, *One match could spark
the whole place.* Like the fire pit

in Turkmenistan, two hundred feet wide
burning since 1971 when geologists,
digging for natural gas

caused a cave-in, tossed in a match
to burn it off. A big *whoosh!*
sent them running.

On the mammogram,
a star-white hole against black,
the size of a pea.

Don't worry, they soothe,
it's probably nothing.
But that nothing *is* something,

a tumor absorbing my light.
And I want nothing
where that something is.

Diagnosis

Melancholy, don't come around here
with your smothering black gloves.
The light you flick here and there
is ash.

Happiness, stay next to me.

See, I've made a place for you on the bench,
where the cherry petals fall slowly.

I'll write: *filament, fireflies in the switchgrass,*
or *honey-colored river ...*

I must take nothing for granted.
Not even my cells, making cancer
of themselves.

The Anointed

The Messiah comes to me in my breast,
the one over my heart.
A little nugget voice, a bead singing.
A lump, size of a small fingernail.
The breast, smeared, tattooed, cut open and radiated:
That voice had to go, leaving a frown for a scar.

Christ comes to me like a stone in the throat,
old glasses in the drawer or a mound
on the road that might be a squirrel
or a glove, palm up, fingers curled.

Comes to me in these Coreopsis, fiercely yellow.
Like the ache when I can't find
words to describe the moonrise,
the sheer redundancy and miracle of it.

Where Did My Mind Go?

I tack up *Lost* posters
describing her as friendly
but with a wild streak.
After weeks, I'm frantic.
Is she sleeping rough?
Busking her way with a uke
and a beat box?

Brochures smelling of salt arrive
from Fiji, the Azores, Catalina.
Each one unsigned,
no *Wish you were here.*

I wait for her on the worn bench
at the corner park
repeating *abandoned*

until the word dissolves
and the day dissolves,
just like the night.

My empire is dull and small.
Forgive the clumsiness
of my feet and hands. My unease with risk.
Without her, I'm forgettable,
though everyone tells me I'm nice.

Hearing My Master's Voice

Some days, I am RCA's terrier
cocking his head:
the needle spins on the wax disc
and out of the brass flower,
my master's voice.
It sounds like Him,
but where is He?

Other times, nothing is shiny.
My legs try to dance a bit,
but they give up.
God is on His knees
washing women's feet.
I think He forgot about me,
the dark thing in the corner,

but if I sit long enough,
a bell will ring in my chest.
Faint, then louder, stronger—
Here I am, you know me—
a voice that will not be unrung.

The Lock Picker

Last night, Christ was under water
trying to pick the lock to my brain.

When I talked, air bubbled up,
distorting His face.

In the morning, I cleaned my pond
of algae and branded my cheeks

with scum from an unconscious
brush of my hand.

That's when I remembered
the sales woman at the Gift Faire

who slid a bromeliad alongside
my display of hand-made cards,

It looks perfect, even though it's on its way out.
Maybe a dying plant is just a dying plant,

but still I pray when I die,
Christ will have picked my lock,

and my door, closed to Him
for decades, will open.

Ikea

> *Wake up sleeper, rise from the dead...*
> —Ephesians 5:14

No clocks. All the windowless walls
gleam with their own light.

Rooms within rooms at first
frightened then lulled her—

Lord, I came here only for a faucet.
How could I have lost You?

She buys a miniature watering can and an indoor-
outdoor rug before hearing the loudspeaker
call her name. *I'm here, Lord, on the 3rd floor*

with the cabinets. The blandness of veneer
is comforting. She wanders to the Malm Queen Size,
stretches out face down.

Christ lifts up the sno-globe
and shakes it, flakes falling on the blue
and yellow building inside. *Wake up! Wake up!*
He says to His flannelled doll on her bed.

The Empty Lot
> *...for I am fearfully and wonderfully made...*
> —Psalms 139:14

So rare in this neighborhood.
Sandwiched between two homes
and bordered by thoroughfares.
Never weed-whacked, never planted,
no raised vegetable garden.
The rickety apple tree at its far end
bears no fruit.

But the robins roost in its crown,
and the crows meander quietly
through the fallow field.

I will not see my body as barren.

I rest my hand
over that empty place and think
about what is beyond my control, this piece of *wild*.
Not what I couldn't be
but how I am made: beautiful.

Saved

My husband and I have Spacebagged our genitalia—
dried kelp bulbs and cowrie shells—
and hung them in the spare bedroom closet.
At Christmas, I nudge them aside
to get to the egg carton of tiny glass:
an angel, lamb, stars.

Cleaning the junk drawer
I tell him, *There's a Swedish woman
who's working on breaking
the human body down into plant food.
Honey, that's what I want
when I die.*

As a Jew, he replies, *I believe
our bodies must not be defiled,*
and writes, *Buy Burial Plots* on the whiteboard.
Well, I say, dumping out old Tupperware,
*as a Christian, we're already dust.
God will remold me after I die.*

We climb the stairs to our bedroom
and pull the eiderdown to our chins.
There are no crashing waves here.
The tide has receded, just dusting
our lips with salt.
Slowly, his hand smoothes my hair.
This is what we have, really:
there's nothing to be saved.

Notes:

"Self Portrait as a Bell" inspired by the poem, "The Healers" by Sophie Collins which first appeared in *Poetry*, vol. CCV, no.1, Oct. 2014.

"I Was Not Mistaken" is inspired by the poetry of Gerald Stern.

"End of the Line" refers to the condition known as Mayer-Rokitansky-Küster-Hauser (MRKH) syndrome, *Characterized by the absence of the vagina, cervix and the uterus...which affects one in every 5,000 women. It is also associated with kidney, bone and hearing difficulties.* www.MRKH.org.uk

"Swiss Border Town in the Time of War" and "View from the Jungfraujoch Railway Café" were inspired by my mother's experiences growing up in Switzerland.

"The White, High-Ceilinged Room" and "Photo of a Slice of an Infant's Face" were inspired by Rosamond Purcell's *Special Cases Natural Anomalies and Historical Monsters*. Chronical Books, 1997.

"Hearing My Master's Voice" references HMV, a trademark and name of a British record Label. The original trademark image features Nipper, a rat terrier, listening to a cylinder phonograph playing his deceased master's voice.

Kate Peper grew up in Minnesota and moved to California in 1994 to work as a free-lance animator in the then-thriving educational games industry. She later went back to school to learn surface and pattern design and for a time designed high-end carpets in San Francisco. Though poetry is a constant preoccupation, she also works on honing her watercolor technique and indulges an unhealthy fascination with gardening. She has taught creative writing as part of California Poets in the Schools as well as to older adults in retirement communities. She lives just north of San Francisco with her husband Bruce and semi-feral dog Hannah.

Many thanks to Leah Maines for choosing this manuscript, April Ossmann for getting the ball rolling, Ellery Akers & Susan Terris for their keen eyes and red pencils, Tom Centolella and our wonderful monthly group of writers, and especially Barbara Swift Brauer and Ann Robinson who were there from the very beginning. A special thanks to Bruce who gave me the support I needed to make this little book happen and my mother who always believed. A shout out of thanks goes to Kim Garcia for being my "Poet in Arms" and Amy Lossie of Beautiful You MRKH Foundation, Inc. for her reaching out. Special thanks also goes to my Faith Community of BayMarin for all my answered prayers.